Little Guides to
Great Lives

VINCENT VAN GOGH

LAURENCE KING

First published in the United States in 2025 by
Laurence King

Published in association with the Van Gogh Museum, Amsterdam

Text by Emma Adams
Illustrations by Jen Khatun

ISBN: 978-1-510-23153-5

10 9 8 7 6 5 4 3 2 1

Printed in China

FSC www.fsc.org MIX Paper | Supporting responsible forestry FSC® C104740

Laurence King
An imprint of
Hachette Children's Group
Part of Hodder and Stoughton
Carmelite House
50 Victoria Embankment
London EC4Y 0DZ

An Hachette UK Company
www.hachette.co.uk
www.hachettechildrens.co.uk
www.laurenceking.com

Other *Little Guides to Great Lives*:
Maya Angelou
Charles Darwin
Leonardo da Vinci
Amelia Earhart
Anne Frank
Stephen Hawking
Frida Kahlo
Ferdinand Magellan
Nelson Mandela

Little Guides to
Great Lives

VINCENT
VAN GOGH

Written by
Emma Adams

Illustrations by
Jen Khatun

LAURENCE KING

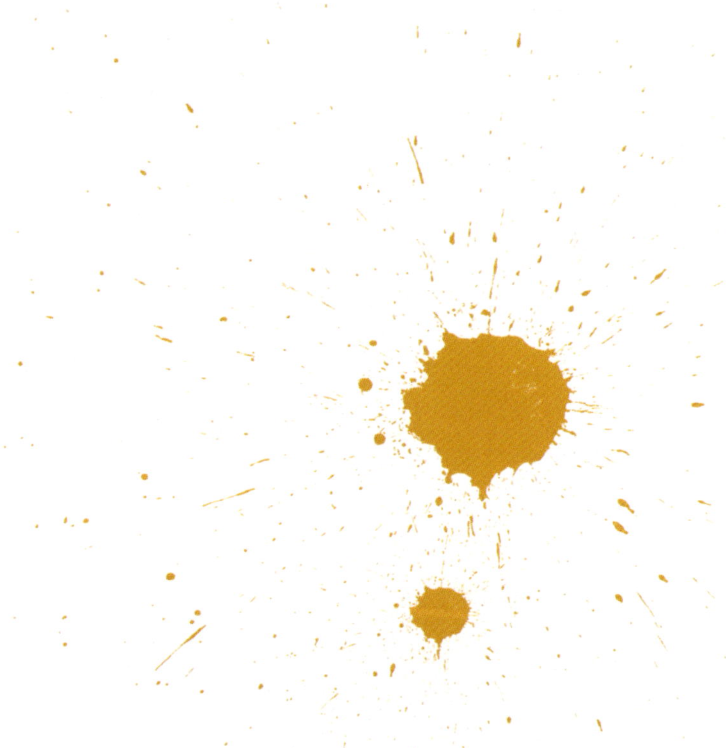

During his lifetime, Vincent van Gogh tried to become many things.
An art dealer.
A teacher.
A preacher.
A painter.
But it wasn't until after his death that Vincent became world-famous and one of the most influential artists in history.

Vincent van Gogh was born on March 30, 1853, in a village named Zundert in the Brabant region of the Netherlands. His father, Theodorus van Gogh, was a Protestant minister and his mother, Anna Carbentus, was a housewife and amateur artist with a talent for drawing.

Theodorus and Anna had six children: Vincent (the eldest), Anna (named after their mother), Theodorus (named after their father), Elisabeth, Willemina, and Cornelis.

As a family, the Van Goghs walked together, gardened together, and even learned history together. Vincent's parents were passionate about sharing not only their country's history, but their own family histories with their children.

Theodorus van Gogh
1822–1885

Anna van Gogh
1819–1907

Vincent van Gogh
1853–1890

Anna Cornelia van Gogh
1855–1930

Theodorus van Gogh
1857–1891

Elisabeth van Gogh
1859–1936

Willemina van Gogh
1862–1941

Cornelis van Gogh
1867–1900

Vincent was a quiet
and introverted child.
He would spend a lot
of his time in nature,
wandering through the
local countryside.

When he was 11, Vincent changed schools, moving from the village school in Zundert to a boarding school in Zevenbergen. He was not very happy at his new school, but he did manage to finish his primary school education.

Open Shed and Farmhouse, Vincent van Gogh, 1864, age 11

When he was 13, he went to a secondary school in Tilburg, but even though he gained good marks at school—especially for languages—Vincent decided to leave halfway through his second year. Then, when he was 16, he went to work for his uncle Cent at The Hague's branch of an art dealer named Goupil & Cie. Vincent was the youngest clerk there.

This letter, written when Vincent was 19, was the first one his brother Theo kept. It marked the start of a remarkable record of their correspondence.

"My dear Theo

Thanks for your letter, I was glad to hear that you got back safely.

I missed you the first few days, and it was strange for me not to find you when I came home in the afternoon . . ."

Vincent to his brother Theo,
The Hague, 29 September 1872

Over the course of his life, Vincent wrote over 2,000 letters; 650 of these were written to Theo, who was his best friend and most devoted supporter. Many of Vincent's letters have survived, which is incredible—they're well over 100 years old!

From 1872 until 1886, Vincent and Theo wrote to each other in Dutch. From February 1888, when Vincent moved to Arles in France, he wrote to his brother in French—and Theo wrote back in French, too.

While Vincent wasn't especially careful with the letters he received—often throwing them away or even burning them—Theo took great care to keep his letters from Vincent safe. And thank goodness he did as many of them are now looked after at the Van Gogh Museum to this day.

Vincent has been described as "a passionate letter writer" who, through his letters to Theo, shared many details of his private life, including his deepest thoughts and personal struggles.

In 1873, Vincent moved to London to work at Goupil & Cie's office there. Around the same time, Theo started working for the company in their Brussels office.

"I imagine you'll like working in the gallery in The Hague, once you've got used to it a little. I don't doubt that your lodgings at the Rooses' will be to your liking.

You should walk a lot if you can find the time."

Vincent to his brother Theo, London,
19 November 1873

While in London, Vincent's interest in art grew as he visited places like the British Museum and the National Gallery to view work by painters such as François Millet and Jules Breton. He was an eager reader, described as reading "everything from museum guides and magazines to literature and poetry."

While in Paris, Vincent became very focused on religion, often including Bible quotes in his letters to Theo.

Vincent would only spend a couple of years in London since in 1875 he was transferred again—this time to Paris. But his time at Goupil & Cie would soon come to an end. Vincent may well have shown a passion for art, but he was less interested in becoming an art dealer—and it seemed that his employers felt the same, because in 1876 they dismissed him.

Vincent travelled back to England in 1876 and took up teaching—first as an unpaid assistant teacher at a boarding school in Ramsgate and then at a private school in Isleworth. Vincent preached at the school and villages nearby but struggled to find new opportunities for himself.

View of Royal Road, Ramsgate, Vincent van Gogh, April–May 1876

Churches in Petersham and Turnham, Vincent van Gogh, 1876

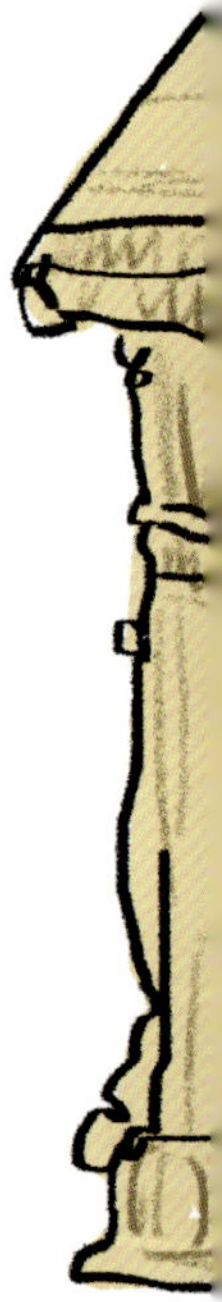

When he went home at the end of 1876 to spend Christmas with his family, he decided not to return to England—a decision that very much followed advice from his father.

In January 1877, Vincent's uncle Cent found another job for him, this time working in a bookshop in Dordrecht. But at 24, Vincent hadn't yet come across a profession that captured his imagination. He was still deeply enthusiastic about religion, so his parents agreed that he could study theology at the University of Amsterdam.

Vincent went to live in Amsterdam with an uncle and started studying for the theology entrance exam—which he needed to take because he hadn't completed his secondary school education.

> "I should really rather like to start making rough sketches of some of the many things one meets along the way, but considering I wouldn't actually do it very well and it would most likely keep me from my real work, it's better I don't begin."

Vincent to his brother Theo, Laken, November 1, 1878

The "Au Charbonnage" Cafe in Laken, Vincent van Gogh, November 1878

But Vincent struggled to focus, and he quit his studies without taking the exam. After a year in Amsterdam, Vincent decided it was once again time to move on, this time to Belgium, where a new profession called to him.

In Belgium, Vincent started working as a lay preacher. He lived and worked in the Borinage, a mining area that was deeply affected by poverty. Vincent would visit the poor, give Bible reading, and also teach.

Coking Factory in the Borinage, Vincent van Gogh, Flénu, July–August 1879

In one of his letters to Theo, Vincent shared his thoughts about the place and the people:

"It's a somber place, and at first sight everything around it has something dismal and deathly about it. The workers there are usually people emaciated and pale owing to fever, who look exhausted and haggard, weather-beaten and prematurely old, the women generally sallow and withered."

Vincent to his brother Theo, Petit-Wasmes, between April 1–16, 1879

1880 was an important year for Vincent, because it marked a complete change of direction in his life—one that his brother Theo had a strong hand in.

Theo, 1880

The brothers were still writing to each other, and Vincent would often send sketches to Theo along with his letters. Seeing Vincent's early talent in these sketches, Theo suggested that Vincent focus more of his energy on his art. Theo was still working as an art dealer, so this was advice that Vincent took to heart.

In October that year, Vincent moved to Brussels, where he took a drawing course at the art academy and started practising drawing and copying artworks from other artists to develop his own drawing technique.

French Peasant Woman Suckling Her Baby (after Dalou),
Vincent van Gogh, Brussels, Winter 1880–Spring 1881

Vincent lived in Brussels until the spring of 1881, when he moved in with his parents again. He could often be found outside, practising his drawing. But Vincent didn't have a job, so Theo, who was now a manager of Goupil & Cie in Paris, decided he would send money to Vincent to help him dedicate as much time as he could to his art.

Vincent's parents didn't quite share Theo's enthusiasm when it came to Vincent becoming an artist, though they did support him as much as they could. But when Vincent and his father had a serious argument on Christmas Day 1881, Vincent moved out of their home and found somewhere new to live in The Hague.

Thanks to the financial help Theo was giving him, Vincent was able to spend his time taking painting and drawing lessons in The Hague with his cousin's husband, Anton Mauve. Anton was an artist—a highly respected artist, in fact—and he taught Vincent to paint in watercolor and oils. Vincent admired Anton greatly.

It was at this time, in 1882, that one of Vincent's uncles paid him to create 12 drawings of The Hague. It was Vincent's first commission! Vincent threw himself into the work and saw it as a great opportunity to develop his craft.

Houses on the Corner of Herengracht-Prinsessegracht, The Hague, Vincent van Gogh, The Hague, March 1882

Seven years later, in 1888, Vincent would paint *Pink Peach Trees in Blossom* and dedicate it to Anton upon hearing of his death. In a letter, Vincent said the painting was "Probably the best landscape I've done."

Vincent created another version of the painting, this one called *The Pink Peach Tree*, and sent it to his brother Theo.

The Pink Peach Tree, Vincent van Gogh, Arles, April–May 1888

Looking at this painting alongside Vincent's drawings from just a few years earlier shows just how much he changed as an artist between 1881 and 1888—something that he no doubt gave credit to Anton for, making his dedication of *Pink Peach Trees in Blossom* all the more touching.

In 1883, Vincent visited Drenthe in the Netherlands. He found the countryside beautiful and was looking forward to drawing and painting the heathland and moors. But he suffered from loneliness and felt isolated there. So, after less than three months, he moved into his parents' new home in Nuenen in December of that year.

Women on the Peat Moor, Vincent van Gogh, Nieuw Amsterdam, October 1883

"Drenthe is superb, but staying there depends on many things—depends on whether one has the money for it, depends on whether one can endure the loneliness."

Vincent to his brother Theo, Nuenen, 6 December 1883

In Nuenen, Vincent worked from a small studio behind his parents' house, then rented a larger studio in the village a few months later. Surrounded by farmers, workers, and weavers, Vincent found many opportunities to paint and draw.

Theo was still sending Vincent money, and Vincent relied on it heavily. He was so grateful for Theo's support that he wanted to repay him somehow—even if he couldn't afford to repay him with money. So, in 1884 Vincent came up with an idea. He would send his paintings to Theo so that they could be sold, and the money from each sale could be kept by Theo as repayment.

Unfortunately, Theo struggled to sell Vincent's paintings. His art just wasn't popular. . . yet!

The Vicarage at Nuenen, Vincent van Gogh, Nuenen, September–October 1885

"Now I have a proposal to make for the future. Let me send you my work and you take what you want from it, but I insist that I may consider the money I would receive from you after March as money I've earned."

Vincent to his brother Theo,
Nuenen, around 15 January 1884

The Potato Eaters, Vincent van Gogh,
Nuenen, April–May 1885

In March 1885, Vincent's father passed away. Not long after this, Vincent moved out of his family's home and into his own studio. It was there that he started work on *The Potato Eaters*—an oil painting that Vincent felt very proud of when he finished it.

What do you think of *The Potato Eaters*?

Despite harsh criticism of the painting at the time, today it's one of Van Gogh's most famous paintings!

In late 1885, Vincent left the Netherlands again and moved to Antwerp, in Belgium.

He would never go back to his homeland.

He began studying at the academy of art in January 1886 and was supposed to stay on until March.

Vincent enjoyed Antwerp at first—especially its museums and churches—but once again, he struggled to earn money and so continued to get by using the funds Theo sent him.

Houses Seen from the Back, Vincent van Gogh, Antwerp, December 1885–February 1886

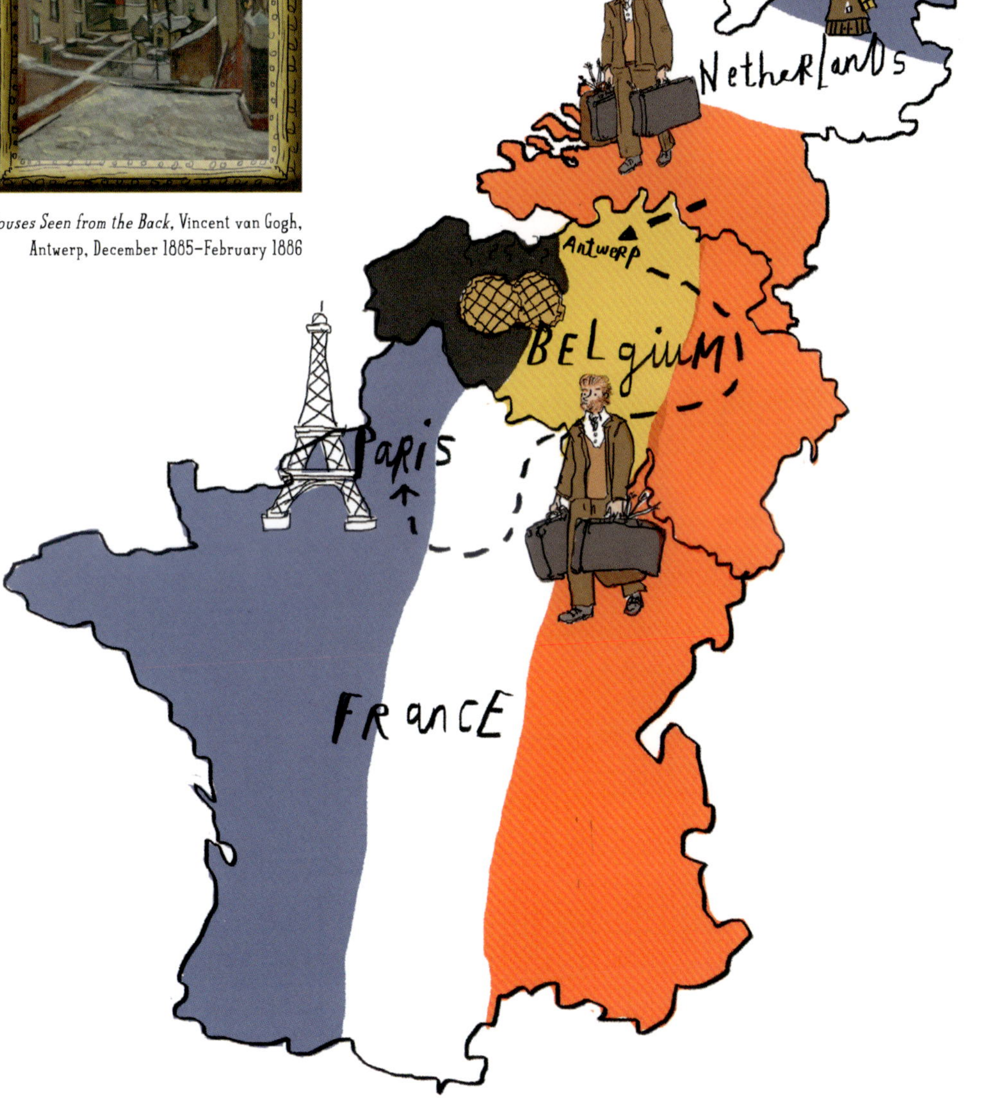

In 1886, Theo was still living in Paris, and when Vincent said that he wanted to move to Paris, too, Theo started looking for somewhere for them to live together. But before he could find them an apartment, Vincent arrived unannounced! Vincent was so eager to take lessons in Fernand Cormon's studio, that his impatience got the better of him.

Fernand Cormon was a French painter and a popular professor who taught many artists who would go on to become known across the world—such as Henri Matisse, Henri de Toulouse-Lautrec, George Hendrik Breitner, and Émile Bernard.

Shoes, Vincent van Gogh, Paris, September–November 1886

Vase with Chinese Asters and Gladioli, Vincent van Gogh, Paris, August–September 1886

"My dear Theo, Don't be cross with me that I've come all of a sudden. I've thought about it so much and I think we'll save time this way."

Vincent to his brother Theo, Paris, on or about 28 February 1886

Portrait of a Woman, Vincent van Gogh, Paris, March–June 1886

Living in Paris made an enormous change to Vincent's art style. Theo introduced him to the work of artists such as Claude Monet, a popular modern artist whose paintings were filled with color, and Vincent was able to work alongside a new generation of artists at Fernand Cormon's studio.

Clearly inspired, Vincent started to experiment, leaving behind the somber palette he'd previously used in his art and instead using brighter, fresher colors.

Vase with Gladioli and Chinese Asters, Vincent van Gogh, Paris, August–September 1886

Small Bottle with Peonies and Blue Delphiniums, Vincent van Gogh, Paris, June–July 1886

The Hill of Montmartre with Stone Quarry, Vincent van Gogh, June–July 1886

Vincent wasn't energized only by the other artists he met in Paris—the city itself gave him so many sights to study and feelings to capture in his art. The toil and struggle he'd witnessed and endured in the Netherlands was replaced by the cafés, boulevards, and bustle of a thriving city.

View from Theo's Apartment, Vincent van Gogh, Paris, March–April 1887

Cafe Table with Absinthe, Vincent van Gogh, Paris, February–March 1887

Montmartre—Behind the Moulin de la Galette, Vincent van Gogh, Paris, July 1887

"Paris is Paris, there is but one Paris and however hard living may be here ... the French air clears up the brain and does one good."

Vincent van Gogh to Horace Mann Livens, September or October 1886

After a year in Paris, Vincent started to experiment with a different style of painting, creating city scenes and portraits using loose brushstrokes alongside the brighter palette he'd been working with. He began to produce more and more work, fueled by the talented artists and the busy city surrounding him. He also started painting sunflowers for the first time—a theme that he would come back to, and build on, in around a year's time.

Vincent and experiments with impressionism

Allotment with Sunflower
Vincent van Gogh, Paris, July 1887

Sunflowers Gone to Seed,
Vincent van Gogh, Paris, August–September 1887

At every opportunity, Vincent tried to sell his art, but except for a few pieces he sold cheaply to art dealers, he was never successful.

For so many years, Vincent had been desperate to learn and grow as an artist, and his time in Paris helped him do this with the financial support of his brother, Theo. But life in such a busy city started to take its toll, and Vincent craved peace, quiet, and the countryside.

So, in February 1888, he left Paris and moved to Arles in the south of France—and later that same year, to the yellow house, a building immortalized by Vincent in one of his paintings.

"It seems to me almost impossible to be able to work in Paris, unless you have a refuge in which to recover and regain your peace of mind and self-composure. Without that, you'd be bound to get utterly numbed."

Vincent to his brother Theo, 21 February 1888

The Yellow House (The Street), Vincent van Gogh, Arles, September 1888

Bold, bright colours, a looser style, and expressive brushstrokes were a big part of the art Vincent created during his time in Arles. He may have only been there for around 15 months, but Arles gave Vincent all the natural beauty, color, and inspiration he was hoping for—and the work he created while he was there is proof of that.

Fishing Boats on the Beach at Les Saintes-Maries-de-la-Mer, Vincent van Gogh, Arles, June 1888

Seascape near Les Saintes-Maries-de-la-Mer, Vincent van Gogh, Arles, June 1888

The Harvest, Vincent van Gogh, Arles, June 1888

In May 1888, Vincent wrote to Theo to tell him of his plan to create an artist's studio in Arles. Vincent called it 'Studio of the South'. He hoped artists would come together there to collaborate and learn from each other, and said that Theo, who was still living in Paris, could sell the works created by artists while they were there.

Vincent to his brother Theo,
28 or 29 May 1888

Theo to his brother Vincent,
Paris, 19 October 1888

In September 1888, Vincent rented four rooms in the yellow house, but only one artist came to stay, and only after a lot of persuasion from Theo. The artist was Paul Gauguin. He was very different to Vincent—in his personality, views, and even the way he worked. The two men would often have disagreements, but they also created some brilliant art in the two months they lived and worked together.

During his stay in the Yellow House, Vincent produced some of what is now considered his most famous work.

Sunflowers, Vincent van Gogh, Arles, January 1889

Gauguin's Chair, Vincent van Gogh, Arles, November 1888

Portrait of Gauguin, Vincent van Gogh, Arles, December 1888

Portrait of Camille Roulin, Vincent van Gogh, Arles, November–December 1888

The Bedroom, Vincent van Gogh, Arles, October 1888

Despite being so productive in his work and despite being proud of what he was achieving as an artist, Vincent's mental health was declining. He would struggle with bouts of depression—as he had done for quite some time.

On December 23, 1888, after a turbulent couple of months living together, Vincent and Paul Gauguin had an explosive argument, and afterward Vincent injured his left ear. Soon afterward, Vincent would be hospitalized in Arles, and during December 1888 and May 1889 Vincent would stay at the hospital three times before transferring to a mental health hospital in Saint-Rémy-de-Provence, where he would end up staying for a year.

The Starry Night, Vincent van Gogh, Saint-Remy-de-Provence, 1888, MoMA, New York

Created for Theo's and Jo's newborn son, Vincent Willem van Gogh

Almond Blossom, Vincent van Gogh, Saint-Remy-de-Provence, February 1890

Throughout all of this, Vincent continued to create art—in fact, he created around 150 pieces of art while he was in the hospital in Saint-Rémy-de-Provence

Outside of the hospital, life went on. Theo married Johanna (Jo) Bonger in April 1889, and they had their first child—a son—while Vincent was in Saint-Rémy-de-Provence. Showing again how much Theo loved his brother, he and Jo named their son after him: Vincent Willem van Gogh.

In early 1890, six of Vincent's paintings were shown as part of a group exhibition of the Belgian artists' association, and *The Red Vineyard* was sold.

In March 1890, ten of Vincent's creations were selected for the annual Salon des Indépendants in Paris.

"How pleased I would have been if you'd been there at the Independents' exhibition . . . Your paintings are well placed and look very well. Many people came up to ask me to give you their compliments. Gauguin said that your paintings are the key to the exhibition."

Theo to his brother Vincent, Paris, 19 March 1890

Though Vincent was fighting a battle with his mental health and was currently hospitalized, his paintings were finally getting attention.

In May 1890, Vincent left Saint-Rémy-de-Provence and traveled to Auvers-sur-Oise. There, Vincent was closer to Paris so could visit Theo more easily, and he once again found the peace and quiet he so desperately needed. He made friends with a doctor named Paul Gachet, who told him to focus on his art. And that is what Vincent did, working at an astonishing rate.

Vincent to his brother Theo,
Auvers-sur-Oise, around 10 July 1890

Wheatfield under Thunderclouds, Vincent van Gogh, Auvers-sur-Oise, July 1890

Vincent did everything he could to help himself get better, and so did the people around him. But unfortunately, he did not get better, and he died not much later. He was only 37 years old.

Tree Roots, Vincent van Gogh, Auvers-sur-Oise, July 1890

When Vincent died, he left behind many who loved him. He also left behind more than 850 paintings and almost 1,300 artistic works on paper. A memorial exhibition of Vincent's work was held six weeks after his death, organized by Theo.

When Theo died just six months after Vincent, he left all the paintings, drawings, and letters his brother had sent to him to his young wife, Jo, and their infant son. Jo decided to honor her husband's memory by continuing his work.

After returning to the Netherlands, Jo organized exhibitions and arranged for Vincent and Theo's letters to be published. She was also able to sell around 200 pieces of Vincent's art to collections around the world. This meant that as many people as possible would be able to see Vincent's work.

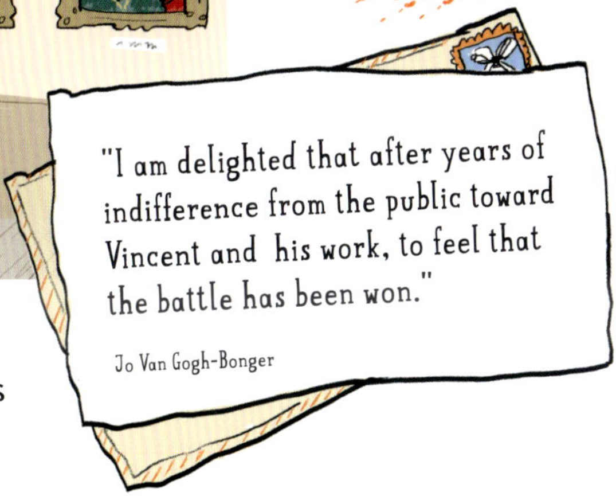

Thanks to Jo's hard work and dedication, Vincent's work was now known across the world.

Jo and Theo's son continued this important work after Jo's death in 1925, transferring the artworks that were still in the family to a foundation. He was also one of the founders of the Van Gogh Museum, which opened on June 2, 1973. It was his greatest wish that the collection be permanently accessible to all, and that Vincent's art continue to inspire everyone, everywhere around the world.

TIMELINE

March 30, 1853
Vincent van Gogh is born in a village named Zundert.

1855–1867
Anna, Theo, Lies, Wil, and Cor van Gogh are born

1860–1867
Vincent's schooling takes place.

1878
Vincent starts working as a lay preacher in the Borinage, Belgium.

1880
Theo advises Vincent to focus on something he's good at—drawing. Vincent moves to Brussels.

1882
Vincent is given his first commission when an uncle pays him to create 12 drawings of views of The Hague.

1886
Vincent takes a drawing course at the academy of art in Antwerp. He moves to Paris to live with Theo, never to return to his homeland again.

1887
Vincent starts experimenting with modern styles of painting, using brighter colors and bold brushstrokes.

1888
Vincent leaves Paris, moves to Arles, and starts an artists' studio in the yellow house. He struggles with depression, and after an argument with Paul Gauguin, he injures his ear.

1891
Theo dies, leaving his collection of Vincent's work to his wife Jo and their infant son.

1905
Jo organizes the largest ever retrospective of Vincent's work.

1914
Vincent's letters are published.

1869

Vincent starts a traineeship in The Hague for international art dealer Goupil & Cie.

September 1872

Earliest record of Vincent and Theo's correspondence.

1877

Vincent goes to live with his uncle in Amsterdam to study for the University of Amsterdam entrance exam.

1883

Vincent visits Drenthe and is inspired by its beauty, but he finds it too lonely and moves back in with his parents a few months later.

1884

Vincent starts sending his art to Theo as a form of repayment for all of Theo's financial help.

1885

Vincent's father dies. He begins working on *The Potato Eaters*.

1889

Vincent is hospitalized multiple times in Arles and on May 8, is admitted to a mental health hospital in Saint-Rémy-de-Provence. He continues working as much as possible.

1890

Vincent leaves Saint-Rémy-de-Provence in May and travels north to Auvers-sur-Oise where he can be closer to Theo in Paris.

July 29, 1890

Vincent dies with his brother Theo at his side.

1973

Van Gogh Museum established in Amsterdam by Vincent's nephew, Vincent Willem.

GLOSSARY

amateur—a person who engages in a pursuit or activity on an unpaid, nonprofessional basis.

art dealer—a person or company who buys and sells works of art, or who helps facilitate the buying and selling of art by artists, galleries, and other interested parties.

clerk—a person who works in an office, court of law, or bank, whose job is to look after accounts and recordkeeping.

collection—a carefully selected set of artworks, connected by artist, theme, or period that is kept together, usually by a gallery or museum for the purpose of presentation to the public.

commission—the request or instruction for an artist to create a specific work of art.

correspondence—written communication between two or more people, usually in the form of letters or emails.

exhibition— a planned, public display of a collection of artworks, artifacts, or other items of interest, often in a gallery or museum.

gallery—a room, building, or other space that is used to display artworks.

Impressionism—a style of painting that started in France in the 1860s that is concerned with producing an "impression" of a scene, by capturing light, color, and movement, rather than an accurate representation of it.

influential—having great power or influence over the way other people think or act.

lay preacher—a preacher who is not ordained in a church or who does not hold a formal university degree in theology.

mental health—a person's cognitive, behavorial, and emotional well-being. It informs how a person engages with and responds to the world around them.

oils—thick, slow-drying paints that are made up of particles of pigment mixed with a drying oil, often linseed oil, that forms a tough, colored film when exposed to air.

palette—the range of colors used by an artist in a single work or a collection of works.

portrait—a picture, usually a painting, drawing, or photograph of a particular person. A self-portrait is a picture an artist creates of their own likeness.

preacher—a person who speaks publicly, often on religious topics, to a group of assembled people.

profession—a paid occupation, or job, especially one that requires formal training or qualifications.

sketch—a drawing or painting that is done quickly and without a lot of detail.

studio—a room or space where an artist such as a painter, photographe, or sculptor works.

technique—a particular way of doing something. In art, this is how tools and materials are used and applied to the artwork to produce particular effects.

theology—the study of religion from a religious viewpoint, often with a focus on the nature of God.

watercolor—a type of paint that can be mixed with water to produce thin, translucent layers of color.

LIST OF WORKS

All artworks, unless otherwise stated:
Vincent van Gogh (1853–1890)
Van Gogh Museum, Amsterdam
(Vincent van Gogh Foundation)

Open Shed and Farmhouse
1864
Pencil on paper
3 3/4 in x 5 1/6 in

View of Royal Road, Ramsgate
Ramsgate
April–May 1876
Pencil, pen, and ink on paper
2 11/6 in x 4 5/16 in

Letter from Vincent van Gogh to his brother Theo with sketch of Small Churches at Isleworth (Detail)
15 November 1876
Pencil, pen and ink on paper

Letter from Vincent van Gogh to his brother Theo
The Hague
29 September 1872
Pen and ink on paper

Letter from Vincent van Gogh to his brother Theo with sketches of Head of a Woman and Head of a Woman (verso)
Nuenen
c. 4 April 1885
Pen and ink on paper

Envelope belonging to letter from Vincent van Gogh to Eugène Boch (recto)
Arles
2 October 1888
Pen and ink on paper

The 'Au Charbonnage' Cafe in Laken
Laken
c. 13 and 15 or 16 November 1878
pencil, pen and ink on paper
10 3/8 in x 14 3/4 in

Coking Factory in the Borinage
Flénu
July–August 1879
Pencil, watercolor on paper
10 3/6 in x 14 3/4 in

French Peasant Woman Suckling Her Baby (after Dalou)
Brussels
Winter 1880–Spring 1881
Pencil on paper
19 in x 10 3/8 in

Bridge and Houses on the Corner and Herengracht-Princesessegracht, The Hague
The Hague
March 1882
Oil on canvas
10 15/16 in x 14 3/8 in

The Pink Peach Tree
Arles
April–May 1888
Oil on canvas
31 7/8 in x 23 11/16 in

Women on the Peat Moor
Nieuw Amsterdam
October 1883
Oil on canvas
10 15/16 in x 14 3/8 in

The Vicarage at Nuenen
Nuenen
September–October 1885
Oil on canvas
13 1/16 in x 16 15/16 in

The Potato Eaters
Nuenen
April-May 1885
Oil on canvas
32 1/4 in x 44 7/8 in

Houses Seen from the Back
Antwerp
December 1885–February 1886
Oil on canvas
7 3/16 in x 13 5/16 in

Shoes
Paris
September–November 1886
Oil on canvas
15 in x 17 13/16 in

Vase with Chinese Asters and Gladioli
Paris
August-September 1886
Oil on canvas
24 1/16 in x 18 1/8 in

Portrait of a Woman
Paris
March-June 1886
Oil on canvas
10 3/4 in x 7 1/2 in

Vase with Gladioli and Chinese Asters
Paris
August-September 1886
Oil on canvas
18 5/16 in x 15 1/8 in

Small Bottle with Peonies and Blue Delphiniums
Paris
June–July 1886
Oil on cardboard
13 9/16 in x 10 5/8 in

The Hill of Montmartre with Stone Quarry
Paris
June–July 1886
Oil on canvas
12 5/8 in x 16 1/8 in

View From Theo's Apartment
Paris
March–April 1887
Oil on canvas
8 1/16 in x 15 in

Café Table with Absinthe
Paris
February–March 1887
Oil on canvas
18 1/4 in x 13 1/16 in

Montmartre: Behind the Moulin de la Galette
Paris
July 1887
Oil on canvas
18 1/4 in x 13 1/16 in

Allotment with Sunflower
Paris
July 1887
Oil on canvas
17 in x 14 5/16 in

Sunflowers Gone to Seed
Paris
August–September 1887
Oil on cotton
8 5/16 in x 10 11/16 in

The Yellow House (The Street)
Arles
September 1888
Oil on canvas
28 3/8 in x 36 in

Fishing Boats on the Beach at Les Saintes-Maries-de-la-Mer
Arles
June 1888
Oil on canvas
25 9/16 in x 32 1/16 in

Seascape near Les Saintes-Maries-de-la-Mer
Arles
June 1888
Oil on canvas
19 7/8 in x 25 5/16 in

The Harvest
Arles
June 1888
Oil on canvas
28 9/16 in x 35 5/16 in

Sunflowers
Arles
January 1889
Oil on canvas
37 3/8 in x 28 3/4 in

Gauguin's Chair
Arles
November 1888
oil on canvas
35 5/8 in x 28 5/8 in

Portrait of Gauguin
Arles
December 1888
oil on jute on panel
15 in x 13 5/16 in

Portrait of Camille Roulin
Arles
November–December 1888
oil on canvas
15 15/16 in x 12 13/16 in

The Bedroom
Arles
October 1888
oil on canvas
28 9/16 in x 35 15/16 in

The Starry Night
Saint-Remy-de-Provence
1889
Oil on canvas
29 in x 36 1/4 in
Museum of Modern Art (MoMA), New York, USA
Acquired through the Lillie P. Bliss Bequest.

Almond Blossom
Saint-Remy-de-Provence
February 1890
Oil on canvas
28 7/8 in x 36 3/8 in

Wheatfield under Thunderclouds
Auvers-sur-Oise
July 1890
Oil on canvas
19 7/8 in x 39 7/8 in

Tree Roots
Auvers-sur-Oise
July 1890
Oil on canvas
19 13/16 in x 39 7/16 in

Translated letter extracts:
Digital edition: *Vincent van Gogh—The Letters*. Ed. Leo Jansen, Hans Luijten, and Nienke Bakker. Van Gogh Museum, Amsterdam & Huygens Institute, The Hague, 2009.
vangoghletters.org